The Goldfinch:
A Guide for Book
Clubs

KATHRYN COPE

CONTENTS

1 - INTRODUCTION

The Reading Room Book Group Guides

This is one of a series of guides designed to make your book group meetings more dynamic and engaging. Packed with information, the Reading Room Book Group Guides are an invaluable resource to ensure that your discussions never run dry.

How you choose to use the guides is entirely up to you. The 'Author Biography' and 'Literary Influences' sections provide useful background information which may be interesting to share with your group at the beginning of your meeting. The all-important list of discussion questions, which will probably form the core of your meeting, can be found in Chapter 8. To support your responses to the discussion questions, you may find it helpful to refer to the 'Themes and Symbols' and 'Character Analysis' chapters.

A plot synopsis is provided as an aide-memoire to recap on the finer points of the plot and clarify the precise sequence of events in the novel. There is also a quick quiz - a fun way to bring your discussion to a close. Finally, if this was a book that you particularly enjoyed, either as a group or as an individual, the guide concludes with a list of books similar in either style or subject matter.

Be warned, this guide contains spoilers. Please do not be tempted to read it before you have read the original book as plot surprises will be well and truly ruined.

The Goldfinch

Donna Tartt does not churn her novels out quickly. Devoted fans of her previous work, *The Secret History* and *The Little Friend* have waited ten long years for her next novel to appear. Most readers will agree that the wait has been more than worth it. *The Goldfinch* is a modern classic, which, like the painting the title refers to, will endure the test of time and bring pleasure to readers for many years to come.

At almost 800 pages, *The Goldfinch* is a great doorstop of a novel; with good reason. A shorter book could not contain the depth of this story or the extraordinary journey it takes the reader upon. It is heartbreaking, funny and clever. As Stephen King so deftly summarised in his review of the novel, it is, "A smartly written literary novel that connects with the heart as well as the mind."

Like all great literature, *The Goldfinch* somehow feels timeless and the influence of classic American and British fiction is evident in Tartt's writing. Her vivid, poetic descriptions are reminiscent of F. Scott Fitzgerald's *The Great Gatsby*, while her witty characterisation bears many similarities to the works of Charles Dickens.

The plot of the novel draws you in and grasps you tight, combining a heart-rending coming-of-age story with a compelling thriller. On finishing it, the reader feels that they have undergone a vast range of experience within its pages. It is a life-enhancing, enriching read.

For book group discussion, *The Goldfinch* raises some weighty philosophical questions. Can immoral actions be justified if they lead to positive results? What makes us fall in love with certain objects and people? Can we trust our hearts to lead us to happiness? And the Big One - how do we lead fruitful lives in the face of impending death?

2 – DONNA TARTT

Born in 1963, Donna Tartt is an American writer who grew up in Missouri. She now divides her time between the Virginia countryside and Manhattan. A very private person, she has a reputation for being enigmatic sparked by her dislike of the trappings of literary celebrity.

Tartt's writing career has proved that dislike of the limelight is not necessarily a barrier to literary success. The publication of her debut novel, *The Secret History*, in 1992 met with immediate success and literary acclaim. A sophisticated psychological thriller, it follows the lives of a group of Classics scholars at a college in New England whose intellectual curiosity leads them to commit murder. Tartt began the novel when she was a student herself and completed it nine years later. Her hard work was well-rewarded when it sold over 5 million copies and was translated into twenty four different languages.

Tartt took roughly another decade to write her following novel, *The Little Friend*. A coming-of-age novel set in 1970s Mississippi, it follows the story of Harriet, a 12-year-old girl determined to take revenge for the death of her brother. Due to the overwhelming success of *The Secret History* and the intervening gap between novels, the publication of *The Little Friend* was much anticipated. Although it was shortlisted for the Orange Prize, for some reason it failed to achieve the mass popularity of *The Secret History*.

A now, almost predictable, ten years later, *The Goldfinch* was published in 2013. Repeating the success of *The Secret History*, the novel has met with universal acclaim from critics and become a bestseller.

The Inspiration for *The Goldfinch*

Tartt's initial idea to begin her novel with an explosion in an art gallery was inspired by a terrorist attack in 2000. The destruction of sixth century Buddhist carvings at Bamiyan in Afghanistan by Islamic fundamentalists prompted the idea of writing about terrorism and the destruction of art.

At the same time, Tartt wanted to include a child who becomes obsessed with a painting in her story. She did not have a specific painting in mind and began searching for an image that would both appeal to a child and be small enough to pick up and 'steal.' In 2003, on a visit to Amsterdam, the author saw a reproduction of "The Goldfinch" by Carel Fabritius and recognised it as perfect for her storyline. Only once she had started writing the novel did Tartt discover the extraordinary coincidence that the artist, Carel Fabritius, died in an explosion.

"The Goldfinch" is an oil on canvas painted in 1654. It shows a life-sized goldfinch tethered to its perch by the ankle with a delicate chain. The painting has been interpreted as a "trompe-l'oeil", composed to deceive the eye so that a viewer standing a short distance away could believe that a real bird was perched there. The depiction of the bird is lifelike and unsentimental. Whilst the chain around its ankle seems dreadfully cruel to our modern day sensibilities, contemporaries of the painter would not find its subject matter unusual. Goldfinches were popular pets in the seventeenth century and were often taught to perform tricks.

The Dutch Master, Carel Fabritius, was a talented pupil of Rembrandt's and went on to become Vermeer's teacher. "The Goldfinch" is one of around fifteen works known to have been painted by Fabritius. It was completed shortly before the artist's tragically early death. An explosion in a gunpowder factory, which devastated much of the city of Delft, killed the artist and destroyed the majority of his paintings. "The Goldfinch" is one of the few that survived.

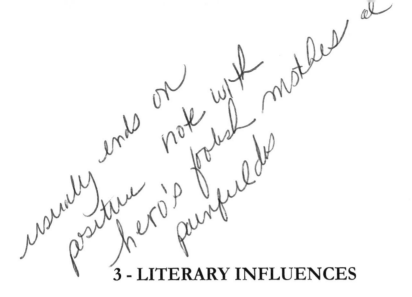

usually ends on positive note with hero's foolish mothers eal punguleds

3 - LITERARY INFLUENCES

Donna Tartt is an exceptionally well-read author. The influence of literary tradition and the work of other classic writers is apparent throughout her work. Tartt's writing is never a pale imitation of what has gone before, however. She takes the best qualities of the work she admires and makes them her own.

THE BILDUNGSROMAN   *bil dunk·   ro män*

The Goldfinch is written in the classic tradition of the bildungsroman. Particularly popular in the nineteenth century, the bildungsroman focuses on character development, tracing the psychological growth of its protagonist. Often beginning with an emotional loss or trauma, the story follows the main character's journey from childhood to adulthood as they go in search of answers to life's questions. Buffeted by the slings and arrows of life, they pass from innocence to experience; their final goal being self- knowledge and emotional maturity.

Charlotte Brontë's *Jane Eyre*, Mark Twain's *The Adventures of Huckleberry Finn*, and any number of Charles Dickens' works (*David Copperfield, Great Expectations, Oliver Twist …*) are all classic examples of the bildungsroman.

Donna Tartt consciously uses this form to engage the reader in Theo's journey. She begins with the fateful day of the explosion at the museum and traces its effect upon Theo over 14 years into adulthood. Like many bildungsroman protagonists, Theo is an orphan and the story follows his attempts to find where he belongs after the death of his mother. His psychological journey is often tortuous and painful but at the end of the novel he has come to a greater understanding of himself and the world.

CHARLES DICKENS

In her rare interviews, Tartt professes a love of the nineteenth century novel and singles out Charles Dickens as one of her favourite authors. Although it has a contemporary setting, there is a strong Dickensian flavour to *The Goldfinch* which goes beyond the use of the bildungsroman format.

The vast range of vividly drawn characters in the novel is very reminiscent of the work of Dickens. The reader is introduced to a breathtaking number of major and minor characters, all written with such painstaking care that the reader is never confused as to who is who. Each character's voice is completely individual.

Like many of Dickens' novels, the plot of *The Goldfinch* is sometimes coincidence driven. Coincidence, as a plot device, is often frowned upon in contemporary fiction. In true Dickensian style, however, Tartt uses it artfully to suggest that human destiny is subject to patterns in life that we have no control over. The discovery that Welty and Theo have so much in common at the end of the novel suggests that some experiences may be preordained (a theory apparently backed up by the coincidences Tartt herself experienced when researching the history of Carel Fabritius).

Orphans and surrogate fathers also abound in *The Goldfinch* - a device frequently used by Dickens, as his 'lost' protagonists find replacement families in their search for self-knowledge.

Although there are similarities to many of Dickens' novels, *The Goldfinch* feels closest in tone and subject matter to the wonderful *Great Expectations*. Like the main character, Pip, in Dickens' novel, who falls in love with icy, Estella, Theo sets his heart upon Pippa, who is equally unattainable. Just as Estella represents the "great expectations" Pip aspires to, Pippa comes to encapsulate the life Theo longs to return to before his mother died. In both cases, their hopes of having their love returned are doomed as Estella and Pippa are deeply damaged individuals. Estella is incapable of love thanks to her dysfunctional upbringing by her crazed guardian, Miss Havisham. Pippa is physically and psychologically scarred by her experience of the bombing. Interestingly, in both novels, the women are in the care of guardians, (Miss Havisham in *Great Expectations*, Hobie in *The Goldfinch*), who take a special interest in the lives of the protagonists. This intensifies both Pip's and Theo's feelings, as it implies a special intimacy between them.

In *Great Expectations*, Pip goes morally astray when an anonymous benefactor, whom he mistakenly assumes to be Miss Havisham, provides the money to make him into a gentleman. Instead of making the most of the opportunity, his new social status goes to his head. Pip shuns Joe Gargery, the man who has been like a father to him, as he begins to find his lack of sophistication embarrassing. Theo behaves in a similar manner when he becomes engaged to Kitsey and is mixing in Manhattan high society. Although Hobie offers Theo the sense of security he has been searching for, he takes advantage of him by placing Hobie's business in danger and betraying his trust. Both characters descend to a humbling all-time low before they can acknowledge their mistakes and become better people.

Theo makes direct reference to *Great Expectations*, mentioning that his new class are reading it when he first moves to Vegas. This is one of several moments when Tartt openly acknowledges her literary debt to Dickens in the novel. Her choice of the deliberately Dickensian sounding names, George Bracegirdle and Lucius Reeve are a sly nod to the influence of the Victorian novelist. Anyone who has read (or seen the film of) *A Christmas Carol* will recognise the parallels when Theo, like Ebenezer Scrooge, wakes up to church bells on Christmas morning and determines to live a better life. The timeless antiques emporium, Hobart and Blackwell, is a tribute to a very similar establishment in *The Old Curiosity Shop* and when he first meets Boris, Hobie admits he had always pictured him as the Artful Dodger in *Oliver Twist*.

THE GREAT GATSBY

Donna Tartt is also an admirer of the great American writer F. Scott Fitzgerald and those familiar with his classic, *The Great Gatsby* may have spotted some similarities with *The Goldfinch*. Again, there is the theme of unrequited love. Jay Gatsby fixates on Daisy, a Southern belle from 'old money', who comes to encapsulate all his dreams. To make himself feel closer to Daisy, he obsessively focuses on the green light outside her home. Theo's mystification of the objects in Pippa's bedroom (old valentines, rosaries, a Wizard of Oz poster) is very similar. Not only does he feel an artificial intimacy with Pippa by looking at her things, he also invests a magic into what are essentially just ordinary objects.

Like Fitzgerald in *The Great Gatsby*, Tartt effectively uses weather conditions to create an often ominous mood. In *Gatsby*, the heat of the summer becomes more and more oppressive as events spiral out of control towards a shocking climax. For more on Tartt's use of atmospheric weather conditions, see the section on 'Location and Mood.'

Tartt's most striking similarity to Fitzgerald is her use of beautifully poetic prose. Fitzgerald was the master of the stunningly poignant description. The concluding paragraphs of *The Great Gatsby* are deservedly well-known because of their powerful summing up of the human condition:

"Gatsby believed in the green light, the orgastic future that year by year recedes before us. It eluded us then, but that's no matter - tomorrow we will run faster, stretch out our arms further ... And one fine morning –

So we beat on, boats against the current, borne back ceaselessly into the past."

Theo's final musings in the last pages of *The Goldfinch* hold that same poetic mixture of loss and optimism, as he describes the struggle of the human spirit to rise above the inevitability of death.

THE IDIOT

Boris's preoccupation with the nineteenth century novel, *The Idiot*, highlights one of the major themes in *The Goldfinch*. Written by Russian novelist Fyodor Dostoyevsky, *The Idiot* tells the story of Prince Myshkin. Myshkin is a kind, compassionate man, but naive and overly trusting of others. Although he tries to lead a morally blameless life, his actions inadvertently lead to murder and disaster.

Boris reads and re-reads *The Idiot* when he is a teenager as he finds its bleak message particularly troubling. If good actions still lead to dire consequences, then what is the point of struggling to live a virtuous life? It is a question that Boris takes very seriously, leading him to believe that the distinction between moral and immoral actions is not always clear-cut. When Boris presents the reward money for "The Goldfinch" to Theo, he refers to *The Idiot*, pointing out that Theo's decision to steal the painting ultimately lead to the recovery of other stolen artworks.

SWANN'S WAY

When Hobie relates the tale of Welty's childhood love affair with art, he makes reference to the early twentieth century novel, *Swann's Way*, by Proust. In this novel, the eponymous hero is captivated by the dishevelled and blotchy-cheeked Odette as she reminds him of a girl in a damaged Botticelli fresco. The incident not only highlights the transformative power of art, but hints at the allure of imperfection or damage. Theo is similarly attracted to Pippa's physical imperfections (her frailty and her limp) as they are signs of the injuries inflicted by the bombing. Just as the antiques that he loves bear visible signs of their history in the wear-and-tear they have sustained, Pippa has her experience written on her body.

MACBETH

Blood is a heavily used motif in Shakespeare's play *Macbeth* and is closely related to guilt. As Macbeth and Lady Macbeth pursue a bloody killing spree in the name of ambition, they appear to be immune from feelings of remorse. We see from their reactions to images of blood, however, how deeply their crimes have affected them at an unconscious level. Macbeth feels as if he is wading through rivers of blood, while, in her famous scene after killing Duncan, Lady Macbeth still sees blood on her hands long after she has scrubbed the last of it away.

In *The Goldfinch*, Tartt draws upon this association to articulate Theo's emotions following the two most traumatic events of his life. During his escape from the museum after the explosion, Theo makes a conscious effort not to look at the dead bodies surrounding him. He still, however, gets blood on his hands as he climbs over the wreckage. Although he showers when he gets home, Theo says that he understands why Lady Macbeth felt the blood was permanently etched on her skin. Similarly, following the shootout in Amsterdam, Theo's face, clothes and glasses are all sprayed with blood. Again, he scrubs himself in the shower and spends the next few days trying to remove the blood from his shirt and coat. In both instances, Theo's reaction is a result of guilt, as well as shock. Theo feels guilty about surviving the museum explosion when it killed so many others, including his mother. In Amsterdam, his remorse stems from committing the ultimate sin of murder.

4 - THEMES & SYMBOLS

Donna Tartt intricately weaves a number of recurring ideas and images (themes and symbols) into *The Goldfinch*.

THE GOLDFINCH

Birds in general keep popping up in the novel. A number of characters are described in ornithological terms. Theo's mother, with her swift movements and alert expression, looks like a bird about to fly away (which of course she tragically does). Pippa is like a small injured bird and Welty, in a childhood photograph, is also birdlike in his fragility. These references all echo the image at the very heart of the novel – "The Goldfinch" by Carel Fabritius. The painting provides a connection between many of the characters. Audrey, Theo, Welty and Horst all fall in love with the image as children and this common bond draws their stories together, connecting the past and the future.

It is, of course, Theo's relationship with "The Goldfinch" which is the most emotionally charged. His initial attraction to the painting develops into obsession as the image of the small yellow bird becomes the centre of his world. He is drawn to it because it was his mother's favourite painting and it almost becomes a mystical representation of Theo's mother after her death. In a life which is now full of uncertainties for Theo, "The Goldfinch" becomes the only constant; timeless and unchanging.

Ironically, although possession of the painting brings Theo comfort, it also haunts him. His illegal possession of it is a constant source of anxiety, but he finds himself unable to willingly give it up. Like the goldfinch in the painting, which is discreetly but firmly chained to its perch, Theo is chained to the picture due to everything that it represents for him. Theo's reaction when he discovers he has been fiercely guarding one of Boris's old textbooks and not the priceless work of art demonstrates how deep his attachment has grown. He experiences no relief in being free of the burden and feels a mixture of despair and shame as he realises how closely his sense of identity is bound up with "The Goldfinch".

THE POWER OF ART

Although Theo's obsession with "The Goldfinch" isn't entirely healthy, it relates to a connected theme – the power of art to speak to the human heart. Theo feels that he has a unique relationship to the painting, echoing Hobie's belief that a great work of art can make the viewer feel as if it were painted specifically for them. Through the connection of Welty's, Audrey's and Theo's childhoods, which are all touched and elevated by the image of "The Goldfinch," the novel demonstrates how art has the ability to speak to us across time. Theirs will be amongst many lives touched by that one particular painting across the centuries. This power, of course, applies not only to art, but great music and literature, also referenced throughout the novel.

NATURE MORTE

The exhibition Theo's mother takes him to see is entitled "Nature Morte." This literally translates to "nature dead," but a more accurate interpretation of its implications would be "death within life." Audrey explains how the subject matter of the Dutch Masters, (ripe fruit on the point of decay, figures holding skulls or hourglasses etc.), expresses the fleeting nature of life. Otherwise known as "vanitas" paintings, they were intended to be a humbling reminder to the viewer of their own mortality.

In *The Goldfinch*, Nature Morte images are not restricted to the art gallery. Theo finds spring in New York particularly depressing, despite its associations with new life. When the daffodils flower and the trees come into bud, it painfully reminds him of the season when his mother died. Similarly, the scent of lilies is inextricably linked in Theo's mind with his mother's funeral and there is a sadly appropriate wilted flower on the front of the condolence card Theo's grandmother sends to him.

The number of unexpected deaths in the novel – Theo's mother; Theo's father; Andy and Chance Barbour - also emphasises the way death forever looms in the background. Theo compares a photograph of Andy and his father with a Nature Morte painting, as their fates appear to be marked out by the objects surrounding them (a model ship, extinguished candles and a clock counting down their allotted time). During his bleakest moments, particularly when he is withdrawing from drugs, Theo becomes fixated on the idea that sickness and death lurk behind everything.

It is not only life itself that is shown to be impermanent in the novel, but everything within it. Friends and loved ones cannot always be relied on (Tom Cable and Kitsey), people are not always what they seem (the mild-mannered Chance Barbour) and old homes can be destroyed to make way for the new.

Although this is a bleak theme, the novel's message is not wholly pessimistic. Whilst Theo is forced to confront the impermanence of life head-on, he comes to believe that it is the struggle to rise above this and carve some kind of meaning out of it that matters. This links back to the other theme of The Power of Art, as the creation, preservation and appreciation of great art allows us to live on in some way beyond our own lifespans.

HEAD VERSUS HEART

Whether it is better to follow your heart or your head in life is one of the weighty questions the novel poses. Theo questions whether the motto, "follow your heart," is a sound one, as the human heart will often lead its owner to pain and even self-destruction rather than happiness.

In *The Goldfinch* there is a clear distinction between those who follow their hearts in life, and those who are ruled by their heads. Boris is the classic example of a character who follows the impulses of his heart. He lives life fearlessly, without questioning whether his actions are wise. At the opposite end of the scale, both Kitsey and Pippa are shown to fear the contents of their own hearts and to consciously turn away from their desires in favour of what is 'good' for them. Kitsey loves the notorious Tom Cable, but determines to give him up, believing that marriage to Theo will provide a more harmonious future. Pippa has feelings for Theo but is aware that being with another 'damaged' individual might prove dangerous to her mental health. She instead chooses the calming influence of Everett, who is unexciting but dependable.

The novel suggests that, for those who are naturally inclined to follow their hearts, trying to follow the more "sensible" path can prove impossible. Theo's father tries to ignore his reckless instincts when he lives at Sutton Place with Theo and Audrey. His attempts to fit into the mould of husband, father and nine-to-five worker leave him bitter and resentful. When he runs off with Xandra to Vegas, he gives in to the call of his self-destructive heart.

In the case of Chance Barbour, it at first appears that he has tamed the wild man within him. The medication he takes for Bipolar disorder enables him to live a "normal" domesticated life. We realise that Mr Barbour's medicated and over-ordered existence has been only a half-life, however, when his obsessive behaviour takes hold again, leading to his (and his son's) death in a manic sailing escapade. Even at his most stable, Chance Barbour is unable to suppress his passion for the sea, and he finally gives in to it entirely. In the case of Larry Decker and Chance Barbour, although their hearts ultimately lead them to disastrous deaths, it is clear that to live in any other way is simply insufferable for them.

Theo remains divided between heart and head, unsure whether it is better to be true to oneself and suffer the inevitable pain or to live a less than full life. For much of the novel, he is seen to follow his heart but, unlike Boris, agonises as he does so. Following his impulses in Vegas leads to Theo's drug addiction and his love for Pippa is also the source of a great deal of pain. When Theo tries to follow his head however, pursuing a relationship with Kitsey, he is left feeling empty at the realisation that they do not really love one another. By the end of the novel, Theo realises that he cannot trust his heart but remains uncertain whether he will honour his engagement to Kitsey or follow Pippa to London.

THE RANDOMNESS OF FATE

The randomness of fate is neatly illustrated in Larry Decker's unsuccessful venture into the world of gambling. Despite the hours he spends working out potential outcomes for baccarat to improve his odds of winning, he is unable to factor in the capricious nature of chance. In *The Goldfinch*, many of the characters are preoccupied with events that have gone wrong in their lives, unable to accept that they were simply the victims of chance or bad luck.

After the bombing, Theo and Pippa fixate on the moment their lives went momentously wrong but are powerless to go back and change it. Both obsess over the series of events leading up to the explosion, blaming themselves for decisions that led them to be there at that particular moment. Similarly, Kitsey feels responsible for her brother's death, wishing that she had gone sailing with her father instead of sending Andy in her place. They all struggle to accept that it was impossible to predict the consequences of their actions.

Of all the characters, Boris is the only one who embraces the randomness of fate. From early on, Boris recognises the sad truth that commendable actions do not always lead to favourable consequences. It is he who points out that the deed Theo feels guilty about for years (stealing

"The Goldfinch") ironically leads to the recovery of a number of stolen masterpieces.

ORPHANS

Even a casual reader will notice that there are a disproportionate number of orphaned characters in the novel. Theo loses his mother and then his father; Pippa is fatherless and her mother dies when she is young; Hobie loses his mother when he is a boy and is estranged from his father and Audrey's parents both die when she is a girl. In almost all cases, it is the loss of the mother which is the greatest source of pain, as fathers are frequently absent or abusive in the novel (see 'Bad Parents' below). The orphaned characters share a sense of displacement and alienation and are forced to venture into the world to find alternative families. Hobie becomes a substitute parent to both Theo and Pippa, and was himself taken under the wing of another surrogate parent, Mrs De Peyster, years earlier.

BAD PARENTS

Appalling parents abound in *The Goldfinch;* particularly fathers. Larry Decker and Mr Pavlikovsky compete for the worst father award, both beating their sons whilst failing to nurture or even feed them. Hobie's father is a sadistic bully who forces his son to work for him without pay. Welty's father abandons his son due to his disability, and his daughter, as she is illegitimate.

Mothers fare only slightly better. Juliet is taken in by Welty when her mother makes it clear she is unwanted. Mrs Barbour prioritises charitable and social engagements over quality time with her children. Only Theo's mother is genuinely caring and warm.

The danger that parental abuse will become a cycle is highlighted in Larry Decker's relationship with his own father, Grandpa Decker. Whilst Larry complains that his father was cruel and physically abusive towards him, he goes on to repeat the same behaviour pattern with his own son, Theo. Consequently, one of Theo's greatest fears is that he will turn into his father. In the case of Welty and Hobie, however, we see that it is possible to break free from learned models of parental behaviour. Although neither have children of their own, the two men become nurturing, 'motherly' figures to those in need of their care.

ADDICTION

Drug addiction is a theme that runs all the way through the novel. Tartt shows its prevalence in every strata of society from the "recreational" use of cocaine amongst Manhattan high-fliers to the overdosing heroin addict at Horst's house. Lying somewhere in between are "self-medicators" like Larry Decker and Xandra who share an addiction to prescription painkillers.

Many of Theo's formative experiences involve drugs. Mrs Barbour gives him unprescribed pills to help him sleep; Pippa's kiss tastes of morphine; Xandra gives him drugs to space him out before they get on the plane to Vegas. From an early age, he learns that when life is unacceptably painful, drugs can make it bearable. This premise is shown to be true, as it is only Theo's drug-taking binges with Boris that make his lonely period of exile in Las Vegas endurable.

Theo's relationship with drugs is related to the novel's other theme of "Nature Morte." He uses drugs as a coping mechanism, but when he comes down from them, his preoccupation with death and mortality becomes almost overwhelming.

5 - LOCATION & MOOD

WEATHER

Weather conditions are described beautifully by Tartt in order to create atmosphere and mood in the novel.

On the day Theo's mother dies, the brewing storm is an omen of the tragic events to come. Ironically, Theo and his mother run into the museum to escape the torrential rain only to encounter something much worse. After the death of his mother, the skies of New York seem to be perpetually rainy, echoing Theo's grief and reminding him of his loss.

In Las Vegas, the oppressive heat and bright sky are in complete contrast to the climate of New York. The vast horizons and harsh light of the desert are a stark reminder of how empty life seems to Theo without his mother and emphasises how far removed he is from his old life.

LOCATIONS

When his mother dies, Theo's sense of having a "home" dies with her. In addition to the wrench of having to leave his childhood home, Theo is acutely aware that there is no one else to take him in who loves him. His choice of the Barbours as temporary guardians is plucked almost from thin air.

Theo's emotional dislocation is reflected in his shifts of geographical location; from New York to Las Vegas to Amsterdam. He remains rootless, feeling unsettled almost everywhere he lives. Consequently, in his letters to his mother, Theo describes the places he is "staying", rather than "living" as everything feels temporary to him. He is also unable to find anywhere that feels right when he and Kitsey are searching for an apartment together.

Each change of location is described in loving detail by Tartt, brilliantly reflecting Theo's state of mind whilst he is staying there.

NEW YORK

Theo is born in New York and it is the city his mother chooses to make her home as a young woman. Before his mother's death, Theo shares her love of the city's bustle and energy. The inscription, "EVERYTHING OF POSSIBILITY" on the Central Park bench where his mother used to sit encapsulates the infinite excitement and promise the city seems to hold. It is by this bench that Theo scatters his mother's ashes.

When Theo's father removes him to Las Vegas, he still thinks of New York as his home. On his return, however, Theo finds the city is not as he remembered it. He perceives it as noisy, dirty and threatening. Even Central Park South, previously a haven of childhood memories, has apparently become a lair for the dangerous and insane as Theo has a disturbing experience with the now unhinged Mr Barbour there and is accosted twice by sinister looking men.

Of course, it is not New York that has changed, but Theo. The city's now nightmarish qualities are a reflection of his state of mind. With his mother gone, it no longer holds the same charm for him and as he suffers from post-traumatic stress, New York's crowded public places become a source of anxiety.

SUTTON PLACE

It is here that Theo lived with his mother and the apartment represents the secure life he had with her before she died. After Theo moves out, he continues to think of it as a perpetual refuge. This begins to change when his father and Xandra desecrate the sanctity of the apartment by rummaging through its contents and selling it off. Theo still takes comfort in visiting the building and chatting to the doormen whom he has known all his life. When he revisits and finds the building an empty shell, ready to be turned into condos, Theo is devastated. Its demolition casts him even further adrift.

PARK AVENUE

This is where the Barbour family's luxurious apartment is located. Like a perfectly arranged stage set, it is elegant but austere. Theo is uneasy in the Barbour's home, feeling that he is somehow messing it up with his very presence. This echoes his feelings within the politely restrained Barbour household generally. Although immensely grateful to them for taking him in, Theo is forever conscious that he is not a family member and has been foisted upon them.

HOBART & BLACKWELL

The Greenwich Village townhouse is the site of Hobie's home, business and workshop. It becomes an enchanted refuge for Theo after his very first visit and some of the most poetic descriptions in the novel are of Hobie's workshop. Literally timeless (as all the clocks in the house declare a different hour), it feels entirely removed from the bustle of modern life. Unlike Mrs Barbour's antiques, which are so carefully staged, they lose all sense of life, Hobie's treasures glow with so much animation that Theo half expects a goat-legged table to start walking around. It is here that Theo realises he loves the patina and history of old things. He comes to associate the smell of beeswax and varnish with a sensation of safety and protection. This is his spiritual home, and it is no surprise that Theo comes to live here after he returns from Las Vegas.

LAS VEGAS

The moment Theo lands in Las Vegas, he is confronted by flashing slot machines, gondolas, the Eiffel Tower, volcanos and showgirls. It is overwhelming in its garish brightness and inauthenticity and Theo immediately imagines his mother's distaste if she were there. Whilst New York was his mother's world, Vegas is his father's chosen domain. Theo notes that while his father looked seedy and inappropriate in New York, he fits in perfectly here.

Theo's sense of dissociation from the real world is heightened in Las Vegas where he feels as if he has landed on another planet. Gone are the cultural diversions of New York. In the barren landscape of the desert, the only things that flourish are the symbols of consumerism: outlet malls, shopping plazas, and supermarkets. Theo finds even the sky is too bright and vast, leaving him feeling exposed after the crowded New York streets he is accustomed to.

Larry and Xandra's choice of home is very much in the spirit of the rest of Las Vegas. A sprawling, mock-Spanish villa on Desert End Road (a grimly appropriate name), it is situated in a deserted suburb, surrounded by empty houses and desert. When Theo discovers the development is called "Canyon Shadows", he naively asks if there is a canyon nearby. Xandra patiently explains that there isn't but, like everything else in Las Vegas, the ranch properties have different "themes."

The interior of the house is even less welcoming than the outside. Little more than a hollow shell, it is made up of overly spacious rooms with virtually no furniture. The air is over-chilled by air-conditioning and the water is excessively chlorinated to the point of being undrinkable. Theo's bedroom is so empty and soulless that he leaves his wardrobe door open, just so that he can look at his clothes. It is little wonder that, at this point in the narrative, possession of "The Goldfinch" takes on an even greater significance for Theo. The age, history and beauty that seem to radiate from the painting are qualities completely lacking in his present environment.

In New York, Theo's grief causes him to feel lonely even though he is surrounded by people. In Las Vegas his state of mind deteriorates due to his physical and social isolation. Canyon Shadows is miles from anywhere and a public transport-free zone. Left to fend for himself for days at a time, Theo's only constant companions are Boris and Popper. At first, it is a relief for Theo to no longer be under the scrutiny of a team of counsellors and the Barbours. It quickly becomes painfully clear, however, that his new "freedom" is the result of nobody caring about what he does. In this environment, the escape route offered by drink and drugs is too attractive to resist.

AMSTERDAM

When Theo arrives in Amsterdam, its ancient streets are as picturesque as a scene from a Christmas card. Theo, however, has descended into a mental abyss, and imbues the European city with his own feelings of doom and despair. He believes it has an "apocalyptic" air with its dark passageways, low skies and murky waters. Theo struggles to orientate himself here, baffled by signs in a language he cannot read and becoming lost for hours in the labyrinth of streets around his hotel. This sense of disorientation is fuelled by the fact that he is completely at the mercy of Boris's 'plan' and out of his comfort zone in this world of serious crime and armed heists.

Theo's sense of unease grows as they travel to the outskirts of the city, where the ancient architecture gives way to an urban wasteland. His sense of foreboding is justified as the straightforward transaction Boris promises ends in a bloody shootout.

Although Theo reaches an all-time psychological low while in Amsterdam, unsuccessfully attempting suicide, it turns out to be his "Damascus." After experiencing a spiritual turning point in his hotel room, he determines to take responsibility for his life. Once he does so, he can appreciate the city's festive charm.

6 - PLOT SYNOPSIS

PART I

It is a few days before Christmas and 27 year-old American, Theo Decker, is alone in an Amsterdam hotel room. He is clearly in hiding from the police as he scans the Dutch newspapers each day for reports of his crime.

Theo dreams of his mother and his memories lead the story back to New York, fourteen years previously. It is April 10th and Theo is thirteen. This, we learn, is the day that his mother died and his life changed irrevocably for the worse.

Theo and his mother, Audrey, are on their way to school for an appointment with the headmaster, Mr Beeman. Theo has been in trouble at school on a regular basis since his alcoholic father left them several months earlier. On this occasion, he has been suspended for loitering with his friend, Tom Cable, while he was smoking. Theo is concerned that Mr Beeman may also have discovered that he and Tom have been stealing small items from empty vacation houses (with the aid of Tom's mother's keys).

Audrey begins to feel queasy in the cab and they disembark before they reach the school. As it is raining, they run into the Metropolitan Museum of Art for shelter. Audrey, a great art lover, cannot resist taking Theo to the exhibition of Renaissance Dutch paintings entitled "Portraiture and Nature Morte." She shows him "The Goldfinch" by Carel Fabritius; a picture she has loved since she was a girl. Theo is captivated by a red-haired girl he glimpses viewing the exhibition in the company of an old man. When his mother moves on to the gift shop, he lingers in the gallery in the hope of speaking to her. Before he can do so, there is an explosion.

When Theo regains consciousness he finds himself in the wreckage of the museum. As he tries to find his way out, he comes across the old man who accompanied the red-haired girl. The old man is dying and seems to mistake Theo for someone he knows. Becoming agitated, he tells Theo to take "The Goldfinch," which is lying amongst the wreckage. He also gives Theo his ring, instructing him to go to Hobart and Blackwell and ring the green bell. Theo takes the ring and the painting and escapes the building. As he leaves, he is confronted by many dead bodies, but none are his mother.

Outside the museum there is pandemonium and Theo discovers the cause of the explosion was a terrorist bomb. Still in shock, he makes his way back home hoping that his mother will be waiting for him there. He spends a terrifying night alone in the apartment trying to find out what has happened to his mother before social workers arrive to inform him that his mother is dead. They explain that they will need to place him somewhere temporarily while they try to make contact with Theo's father or grandparents. Theo asks them to contact the parents of Andy Barbour, an old school friend whom he no longer socialises with. Theo and Andy became friends when they were both bullied after being singled out as gifted at school.

The Barbours agree to Theo staying and he goes to live with them in their intimidatingly perfect apartment on Park Avenue. Although Andy is pleased to have Theo's company and Mr and Mrs Barbour are perfectly courteous, the other Barbour children are hostile towards Theo and he feels uncomfortable living there.

When he returns to school, Theo is hurt to discover his previous friend, Tom Cable, now avoids him. A card arrives from Theo's paternal grandparents in Maryland making it clear that they are unwilling to take in their grandson but suggesting he could stay in a Holiday Inn nearby. His father cannot be traced.

Theo is questioned by the police about the day of the explosion. He is on the verge of confessing that he took the painting, which he has left hidden at his old apartment, when he realises the police have no idea which room he was in when the explosion took place. He keeps quiet.

Theo begins to dwell on the instructions the old man in the museum gave him. He locates an antiques dealer in Greenwich village called Hobart and Blackwell. When he rings the green bell, he is greeted by James Hobart (Hobie). Theo presents the ring to Hobie but does not mention the painting. He learns that the old man in the museum, Welty Blackwell, was Hobie's business partner and is saddened when Hobie confirms that Welty died in the explosion. On asking after the girl who was with Welty, Theo discovers that her name is Pippa. She survived the bombing but her leg was very badly broken and she also sustained a serious head injury. As Welty was Pippa's Uncle and guardian, she still lives at Hobart and Blackwell with Hobie. When Theo meets Pippa again, she appears to recognise him, although she has suffered a great deal of memory loss. Hobie invites Theo to call in again.

Still overwhelmed with grief at the death of his mother, Theo is finding his regular sessions with a psychiatrist of little help. When he wants to escape from the pain of reality, he thinks about Pippa and the sense of refuge he felt at Hobart and Blackwell. He is devastated when he discovers that Pippa's Aunt Margaret is taking her to live in Texas. When he goes to say goodbye, Pippa kisses him – a moment that he will replay in his mind many times.

Despite the absence of Pippa, Theo continues to visit Hobie in his workshop and takes pleasure in helping him with restorations. He worries about his continued possession of the painting but cannot bring himself to do anything about it. Things appear to be looking up for him when he reads in a newspaper that "The Goldfinch" is believed to have been destroyed in the bombing. He is also delighted when the Barbours ask him to go to Maine for the summer with them - an indication that he might be able to stay with them permanently. To Theo's dismay, however, his father, Larry, unexpectedly arrives with his girlfriend Xandra to take him to Las Vegas.

Theo reluctantly accompanies his father and Xandra to the old apartment in Sutton Place. While his father and Xandra sort through Audrey's possessions, Theo retrieves the painting before they discover it and asks Jose, the doorman, to store it in the package room. Jose informs Theo that several men have been enquiring about his father's whereabouts, trying to retrieve debts. The doormen also present Theo with some money claiming that Goldie borrowed it from his mother.

PART II

Before he leaves for Las Vegas, Theo retrieves "The Goldfinch" and takes it with him.

It soon becomes apparent to Theo that his father was leading a double life when he was married to his mother and his "business trips" involved visiting Xandra in Vegas. He also learns that his father is not teetotal, as he previously claimed, but has replaced his addiction to Scotch with a reliance on Corona Lights and prescription drugs. He makes his money from "professional" gambling.

Theo's new home is a sprawling new build in 'Canyon Shadows,' a deserted suburb, miles from anywhere. He is left alone for days on end, often with very little food, while his father and Xandra stay at the Strip.

When Theo starts school in Vegas, he quickly makes friends with Boris, an Eastern European boy who lives in Canyon Shadows. Boris is also motherless and neglected by his wealthy but abusive father. Theo and Boris spend almost all their time together, talking, smoking, shop-lifting, drinking and experimenting with drugs. Their drinking and drug-taking sessions become increasingly extreme, sometimes leading to sexual intimacy between the two boys and occasionally erupting into violence. The dynamics of their relationship change however when Boris meets his girlfriend, Kotku.

Theo feels increasingly lonely as Boris spends most of his time with Kotku. Meanwhile, Theo's father begins to show more interest in him, claiming he wants to make up for his past failures. He tells Theo he intends to open a savings account for him and asks for his social security number.

While Theo is alone in the house, he receives an unsettling visit from Bobo Silver; a man his father clearly owes money to. Theo concludes that "The Goldfinch" may not be safe in his father's house and transfers it to his locker at school.

Shortly afterwards, Theo's father announces that he wants to give up gambling and start up a restaurant business. Larry instructs Theo to ring his mother's solicitor, Mr Bracegirdle and ask him to wire $65,000, pretending it will go towards private school fees. When Theo questions this request, his father punches him in the face and threatens to assault him again if he doesn't make the call. Mr Bracegirdle informs Theo (and his listening father) that under the terms of the account, the money would have to be sent directly to the private school rather than to Theo. He also tells Theo that an unauthorised party has fraudulently attempted to take money out of the account his mother set up for him. On learning that he cannot access the money, Theo's father has a breakdown.

Boris asks Theo to run away with him, as his father is leaving for Russia via Australia and plans to take Boris with him.

Bobo Silver pays a return visit to the house, accompanied by a Russian heavy with a baseball bat. He warns Theo that if his father doesn't pay his debt his next visit will be less pleasant.

Xandra returns from work and breaks the news that Theo's father has been killed in a drunken collision with a tractor-trailer. Theo realises that he will have to leave before Social Services arrive and agrees to run away to California with Boris. When Xandra passes out from a combination of drink and drugs, the two boys steal money and a large cache of drugs from her bag. Theo also discovers a pair of his mother's emerald earrings which his father evidently stole from her. Although Theo is impatient to leave immediately, Boris is oddly reluctant, trying to delay their departure. Unhappily, Theo resolves to leave without him.

Theo travels to New York by bus, concealing Xandra's neglected dog, Popper, in a bag. He becomes increasingly ill as the journey progresses. When he finally arrives in New York, the city appears more hostile than he remembers it. Hoping that the Barbours will take pity on him, he makes his way to their apartment but, *en route*, bumps into Mr Barbour in Central Park. Andy's father clearly does not recognise Theo and violently rebuffs him. In desperation, Theo decides to try Hobie. Despite Theo's failure to reply to his last few letters, Hobie greets him with genuine pleasure and Theo is delighted to discover Pippa is also staying there.

At Hobie's insistence, Theo calls Xandra who comments on the similarities between Theo and his father. Although Theo denies they have anything in common, he is secretly haunted by the belief that he shares many of his father's character defects.

PART III

As Hobie nurses him back to health, Theo worries that excessive drug use has damaged his body and brain. He receives a few texts from Boris indicating that he has prospered since Theo left by selling Xandra's drugs to the rich kids at school.

Theo speaks to Mr Bracegirdle again and discovers that he could have accessed the money in his savings account but the solicitor didn't release it as he suspected Theo's father was behind the request. Distressed at the knowledge that his father's death could have been prevented, Theo falls ill again.

Pippa returns to boarding school and Mr Bracegirdle, while agreeing that Hobie should assume unofficial guardianship of Theo, suggests that boarding school would be the best option for him in the long term. Desperate to remain with Hobie, Theo applies to an elite college program in the city, cramming obsessively for the entrance exams. He accompanies Hobie almost everywhere.

Theo's anxiety about still possessing "The Goldfinch" deepens. He learns from a newspaper report that three of the paintings initially believed to have been destroyed in the museum bombing have been recovered from thieves. The thief who has been captured was a paramedic called to the scene of the explosion. He and his accomplices were expected to receive sentences of approximately twenty years. Theo is concerned that he may be reinvestigated and that Hobie will also go to prison if the painting is found on his property.

Meanwhile, Theo is accepted onto the elite college program. Although he realises he is lucky to have got in, Theo finds it impossible to relate to the other students and makes minimal academic effort. Feeling that his home with Hobie is insecure, Theo attempts to make himself indispensable, learning the art of antiques restoration. One day he accompanies Grisha, an employee of Hobie's, to the storage unit Hobie uses. Theo is astonished at the number of pieces Hobie has simply sitting in storage. Grisha agrees and claims that, as Hobie isn't interested in making money, the business will soon be bankrupt if he doesn't get someone to run the shop for him.

Inspired by the visit, Theo transfers "The Goldfinch" to a storage unit for safe keeping. On the way home, he decides to call in on the doormen at Sutton Place. When he arrives, he is devastated to discover that the building is an empty shell, destined to be transformed into luxurious condos.

PART IV

The story skips forward to eight years later. Unimpeded by his failure to graduate from college with distinction, Theo has become a partner in Hobart and Blackwell. While Theo runs the shop, Hobie continues to concentrate on restorations.

Theo is stopped in the street by Andy Barbour's brother, Platt. He breaks the news to Theo that both Andy and his father recently died when their yacht capsized. Theo agrees to visit Mrs Barbour with Platt. He is shocked to discover that grief has destroyed Mrs Barbour's air of cool elegance and turned her into a virtual recluse. She is delighted to see Theo and he promises to return on another occasion for dinner. Platt mentions to Theo that his sister Kitsey sometimes sees Tom Cable and implies Tom has turned out badly, having been caught stealing from clubhouses on an number of occasions.

Theo struggles to come to terms with Andy's death. He is also anxious about a client who is refusing to be placated after Theo knowingly sold him a fake chest-on-chest.

For some time, Theo has been passing off Hobie's "changelings" (pieces beautifully cobbled together from several others) as originals. Hobie is unaware of Theo's scam and on the occasions when the deception has been discovered by the client, Theo has bought the pieces back, and in so doing gained provenance for the piece, raising its value for resale. The scheme has proved highly profitable. The present client, Lucius Reeve, is insisting that Hobie knowingly produced the piece as a forgery.

Theo is still using a concoction of drugs which he believes help him to function. After running out of the supply stolen from Xandra, he now buys them off the street. On occasion, he has attempted to quit but finds the deep depression that accompanies withdrawal intolerable. Still in love with Pippa, he eagerly anticipates her next visit. He is, therefore, bitterly disappointed when she returns from London with Everett, her English boyfriend.

When Platt Barbour asks Theo to sell some of his mother's antiques without her knowledge, Theo glimpses an opportunity. Guessing that Platt needs money, he refuses to sell the furniture but instead pays Platt for fake provenance documentation stating that the fake chest-on-chest he sold to Lucius Reeve was once part of his mother's collection.

Theo meets with Lucius Reeve, confident that the fake documentation will appease him. He is horrified, however, when Reeve shows no interest in the document and accuses Theo of stealing "The Goldfinch." Reeve knows the story of Theo's arrival at Hobart and Blackwell with Welty's ring and realised this could only mean he was in the same room as "The Goldfinch" when it disappeared. He shows Theo a newspaper article about a botched FBI raid in Florida. "The Goldfinch" was believed to have been used as collateral in a drugs trafficking deal but hadn't been recovered from the scene of the raid. Reeve believes that Hobie is also in on the theft and has concluded that he and Theo are farming it out to raise collateral. He offers to buy the painting from Theo for half a million dollars. When Theo denies everything, Reeve threatens to inform the art-crimes division of what he knows. Perplexed by the article, Theo believes a forgery of "The Goldfinch" must be circulating in the art underworld. He is aware, however, that if the police discover, as Reeve has, that he left the museum with Welty's ring, they will quickly realise which gallery he was in.

Forced into a corner by Reeve, Theo tells Hobie an edited version of the truth. He claims that Reeve paid seventy-five thousand dollars for a piece Theo claimed to be an Affleck but has refused Theo's attempts to buy it back. Theo admits that it is not the only piece he has sold under false pretences but lies to Hobie about the number of customers he has defrauded and the length of time he has been doing it for. Hobie tells Theo that in order to safeguard the reputation of the business, he must contact everyone he has sold fake pieces to, explain that there are doubts over their authenticity and offer to buy them back for their original price. Theo agrees, knowing that they do not have enough money to reimburse every defrauded client. His unease grows as he discovers from a news article that the frame of "The Goldfinch" has been found intact. He also suspects that he is being followed by one of Reeve's henchmen in the hope that he will lead them to the painting.

Theo has become engaged to Kitsey Barbour. To Mrs Barbour's delight, they quickly became romantically involved after Theo's first dinner with the Barbours. Theo has thrown himself into the relationship, realising that his obsession with Pippa will only ever lead to unhappiness. As they look for an apartment together and prepare for their high society wedding, Theo briefly starts to feel much happier but then slumps into depression again. Although he has enjoyed the early days of he and Kitsey's romance, he is uncomfortable with the relentless pace of their social life as a couple. He also dreads his fraudulent activities becoming public before the wedding.

Lucius Reeve has been sending threatening letters; one of them addressed directly to Hobie. Theo lies to Hobie, claiming that Reeve is trying to pressure him into fraudulent activities. His anxiety increases when Grisha tells him that the shop is being watched and an unidentified man has been asking questions about Theo.

Since his relationship with Kitsey began, Theo has resisted taking drugs but has been drinking heavily to compensate. As his anxiety reaches a peak, however, he craves drugs. Unable to contact his old drug dealer, he wanders the streets hoping to find somewhere to buy them. Here, he bumps into Boris whom, we learn, is the disreputable looking man who has been watching the shop and asking questions about Theo. Boris is accompanied by a mysterious female companion called Myriam. He also has his own driver. Boris is evasive over where he lives now and what he does for a living. He tells Theo that he became seriously addicted to the pills they stole from Xandra and that he lived with Xandra for a few months when his father went back to Australia. After making a lot of money dealing drugs at school, he paid back the money he had stolen from Xandra. Boris insists that he owes his success to Theo and asks him to come and work for him.

Theo takes Boris to Hobie's to reunite him with Popper. Boris then takes Theo to a Russian club and other dubious haunts in a drug-fuelled drive around New York. Boris tells Theo that he went on to work for Bobo Silver at the point when his drug dealing at school was about to be exposed. He repeatedly apologises to Theo for his actions and Theo finally realises that Boris stole "The Goldfinch" from his school locker in Las Vegas. Too stunned to react, Theo abruptly leaves.

The following day, Theo goes to the storage facility where he keeps "The Goldfinch." Inside the package he finds Boris's old Civics textbook from school. Although he knows he should be relieved to be free of the painting, Theo is overcome with humiliation and self-disgust. He panics, realising he left Popper in Boris's car and wonders how he can get him back without alerting Hobie to his absence. Boris arrives at the shop with Popper. He explains that he used the painting as collateral for various "deals" and believes it is somewhere in Europe. He vows he will try to get it back for Theo.

A few days later Theo travels uptown with Boris to visit a man called Horst, who may have information about the painting. Boris explains that the deal in which the painting was lost was made through Horst's associate, Sascha. Boris only received half of the goods promised from the deal and the gang were arrested without the picture being retrieved.

Horst's townhouse is a surreal mixture of grandeur and decay and the floor is a mass of semi-conscious drug addicts. Horst tells them that Sascha believes the painting is now in Ireland. Boris and Theo swiftly depart when a young man collapses from an overdose and the other residents of the house are attempting to revive him. Boris suspects that Sascha may be responsible for engineering the police raid so that he could disappear with the painting.

On the way home, Theo calls in at Kitsey's apartment. He knows that she is out for the evening but decides to let himself in and wait. When he arrives, he finds the chain on the latch and Kitsey's roommate, Emily, refuses to let him in. As Theo attempts to call Kitsey, he sees her across the street in the arms of Tom Cable. From Kitsey's body language, it is clear she is in love with him. Although Theo had not suspected Kitsey of having an affair, on reflection, he realises that the signs were obvious. He also realises that the rest of the Barbour family know and disapprove of Tom.

When Theo confronts Kitsey about her affair, she at first denies it and then confesses claiming she didn't think it mattered until they were married. Kitsey questions Theo over whether he is truly as upset as he claims to be. She reveals that she knows about his drug habit and argues that their marriage will be a stabilising force for both of them. When Theo presses her, Kitsey admits that their impending marriage is a decision of the head and not the heart. Theo privately admits that his feelings for Kitsey are not as strong as he would like them to be. Nevertheless, he agrees with Kitsey that there is no need for them to go their separate ways.

Pippa returns for a visit and agrees to go to the cinema with Theo. They watch a documentary about the pianist, Glenn Gould, and, during the film, Pippa becomes distressed. Theo learns that she is still struggling to accept that her ambition to be a professional musician was thwarted by the neural damage she suffered in the bombing. For the first time, he realises that Pippa is as damaged by post-traumatic stress as he is.

Theo arrives at his lavish engagement party and finds a room full of people he doesn't know. Mrs Barbour introduces him to Havistock Irving, who claims to be an associate of Lucius Reeve. Irving clearly knows about his theft of "The Goldfinch" as well as all the details of Theo's fraudulent sales. Hobie recognises Irving as 'Sloane Griscam;' a fraudster who charmed his way into the houses of elderly people to rob or cheat them of their valuables. Hobie and Welty testified against Griscam and his partner, 'Lucian Race' more than thirty years previously. Race disappeared before the trial but Griscam was sent to jail. Boris arrives at the party and tells Theo to go home and get his passport and all the money he has access to. Theo leaves the party with Boris, telling Kitsey he has to go away for a few days on business.

PART V

Theo takes all the unbanked cash from Hobart and Blackwell's cash register. He also leaves a note in Pippa's boots declaring his love along with a first edition of *Ozma of Oz* and an eighteenth century topaz necklace. He and Boris are to take separate flights to Antwerp where Boris has an apartment. Gyuri, Boris's driver, will then take them to Amsterdam, as Boris believes Sascha has taken the painting there.

When they arrive in Amsterdam, Theo takes a room in a hotel while Boris stays at a girlfriend's flat. Boris tells Theo he is to pose as a rich American who wants to buy "The Goldfinch." Theo is uncomfortable with the plan but Boris dismisses Theo's alternative idea of making an anonymous call to the arts-crime division.

Boris's men set up a meeting at the Purple Cow Café. On the way to the meeting, Boris and Theo change cars and Boris locks their passports in the glove box of the first car for safe keeping.

At the Purple Cow Café, two men are waiting for them. During the transaction, Theo realises that Boris and his men, Victor Cherry and Gyuri are armed. Before Theo hands the money over, Victor stuns one of the rival gang with the butt of his pistol and retrieves the painting from a broom closet in the kitchen. Theo makes his escape with Boris, Victor and Gyuri, still in possession of the money. As they do so, Theo glimpses an Asian boy also fleeing from the scene.

Safely back in the car, Boris tells Theo that Victor's attack had been improvised, taking advantage of the fact that the third man who was supposed to be involved in the transaction did not appear. Victor claims that they had a lucky escape, as he found a sawn-off shotgun in the kitchen when he retrieved the painting.

When they return to the garage to transfer back to their original car, Boris insists that his men, Victor, Gyuri and Shirley drive off with the money which will be divided later. Before Boris and Theo can also leave, however, they are confronted by two armed American men, accompanied by the Asian boy from the Purple Cow Café. Boris recognises the men as Martin and Frits, who work for Horst. Horst's men retrieve the painting and take Boris and Theo into a dark corner of the garage to shoot them. Boris creates a diversion and shoots Frits in the head but only succeeds in wounding Martin. Martin retaliates by shooting Boris in the arm. As Boris lies wounded on the floor, Theo picks up his gun and shoots Martin dead. In the ensuing chaos, the Asian boy escapes the scene with the painting. Boris plants drugs at the scene to make it look like a drugs deal gone wrong.

Theo drives them back to Amsterdam where they become gridlocked in traffic travelling into the city centre. Boris says he may have to leave town for a while but will contact Theo at the hotel as soon as he can. Theo gets out of the car and makes his way back to his hotel, covered in blood.

Back in his hotel room, Theo unsuccessfully tries to scrub the blood out of his clothes. He drifts in and out of consciousness after taking the potent dope that Boris gave him before they parted. When he fully awakes, he realises he is feverish and ill.

As he waits for news from Boris, Theo loses all track of time. He checks the Dutch newspapers in the hotel which show photographs of the garage where he killed Martin, and recognises the Dutch words for "drugs" and "murder." Intending to call Boris, he short-circuits his cell phone trying to charge it.

Theo panics as he realises his passport is still in Boris's car and he is unable to get home without it. He ventures out of the hotel to Centraal Station but finds he is unable to buy a ticket without his passport. Calling the United States Consulate of the Netherlands, he claims that he needs to travel home but his passport has been stolen. As it is Christmas Eve, Theo is horrified to discover the Consulate is closing early and will not be open again until the Monday after Christmas. A new passport will then take a further ten working days to process.

Theo returns to his hotel and decides to commit suicide. After writing farewell letters to Hobie, Mrs Barbour, Pippa and Kitsey, he takes aspirin with wine but his stomach rebels and he is almost immediately sick.

That night, instead of his usual dream where he unsuccessfully searches for his mother, Theo clearly sees her for the first time since she died. He wakes just as she is about to speak to him. Theo interprets the dream as a visitation from his mother and believes he can still feel her presence. He hears church bells, heralding Christmas morning and feels he has reached an epiphany. Theo decides that he is going to face up to the consequences of his actions and turn himself in at the American Consulate.

Before Theo can leave the hotel, Boris arrives with a bag full of money. Suspicious of where it has come from, Theo refuses to accept it and remains determined to hand himself in. Finally, Boris reveals that the money is a portion of the two million euro reward for information leading to the recovery of "The Goldfinch." He also informs Theo that Sascha is now in jail and that many other important stolen works of art were recovered in the raid, including works by Rembrandt and Van Gogh. Boris returns Theo's passport and invites him to stay at his home in Antwerp for a while before he flies home.

Theo stays at Boris's apartment for two days recuperating from his illness before flying to New York. When he returns, Hobie is uncharacteristically guarded with Theo and clearly no longer trusts him. He reprimands Theo for giving Pippa such a valuable necklace on the night of his own engagement party and informs him that Lucius Reeve has told him about the true scale of the antiques frauds and about the theft of "The Goldfinch."

Theo finally tells Hobie the whole story, only excluding the deaths of Frits and Martin. He fully expects that Hobie will want him to leave but Hobie stops him and produces a photograph of Welty as a boy with a reproduction of "The Goldfinch" in the background. Hobie explains that Welty grew up surrounded by paintings when he was a child in Cairo and they held great significance for him. When Welty's father banished him to America because of his disability, he keenly felt the loss of their beauty and travelled widely to see the originals. On the day of the bombing, he had specifically taken Pippa into the museum to show her "The Goldfinch."

The story skips ahead to a year later. Theo is travelling the world, buying back the fake antiques he sold to clients. The story he has related, we learn, is the result of a series of letters he wrote to his mother after her death.

Theo is at a crossroads in his life. He continues to visit the Barbours when he is in New York and his engagement to Kitsey has not been called off. He also considers the possibility of visiting Pippa in London, despite the fact that Pippa has made it clear that they are both too badly damaged to be good for one another. While he acknowledges the truth in this, Theo wonders if he is capable of changing and becoming the strong one in the relationship.

Theo reflects on whether it is better to live like Kitsey and Pippa and consciously turn away from self-destructive desires, or to be like Boris and embrace the impulses of your heart, even if the inevitable consequence is pain. He suggests that ultimately, the best we can do is to live life as fully and joyfully as possible, despite the certain knowledge that death awaits every one of us.

7 - CHARACTER ANALYSIS

One of the joys of reading *The Goldfinch* is encountering its huge cast of brilliantly drawn characters. Tartt covers the whole range of society from Manhattan socialites to doormen and underworld fixers. No matter how brief their appearance in the novel, Tartt puts equal energy into every one of them, capturing their dialect, mannerisms and quirks of appearance so sharply that we feel we would instantly recognise them if we met them in the street.

Theo Decker

Theo is the first person narrator of the novel, and we navigate the story of *The Goldfinch* through his eyes. His journey takes him from mild delinquency to grifting drug addict and finally murderer. Although, as readers, we are frequently frustrated by his actions, we never lose our empathy for him.

Theo has already encountered disruption in his family life before the novel begins. His unpredictable, alcoholic father has left several months earlier. With the death of his mother, however, Theo's life is turned upside down and he becomes a virtual orphan. His mother was the only person in Theo's life who provided unconditional love and a sense of security. Without her, he loses all sense of rootedness.

Theo's grief at his mother's death is incredibly complex and impacts on his life way into adulthood. It is intertwined with guilt, as the trouble he was in at school led Theo and his mother to be in the museum at the time of the explosion. Theo describes a sense of dissociation, as if his soul is no longer connected to his body. He is also acutely aware that every life experience he has widens the distance between him and his mother. This reluctance to fully participate in life is shown in his lack of effort in academic studies (despite great aptitude) and his casual relationships with women who are already committed to other men. Even when Theo begins dating Kitsey, although he convinces himself he has made an emotional commitment to her, he has subconsciously chosen someone who is emotionally involved elsewhere. When he discovers Kitsey's affair with Tom Cable, Theo is forced to admit that his feelings for her are not as intense as they should be.

In contrast to Theo's lack of commitment to life generally, he emotionally overcommits in other areas. At the beginning of the novel he mentions his tendency to "fixate" on strangers, investing them with certain qualities in his imagination. Theo's longing for his mother leads him to fixate on two objects in particular: the painting of "The Goldfinch" and Pippa.

"The Goldfinch" is linked with his mother in so many ways that Theo becomes almost unable to distinguish between the two. It is an image she loved since childhood; Theo's last moments with her were spent looking at it and Theo is even reminded of her birdlike mannerisms when he looks at the delicate goldfinch in the painting. Significantly, he has also been able to "save" the painting, as he was unable to save his mother. Just like the chained goldfinch, Theo is chained to the painting because of what it represents to him and it becomes both a blessing and a curse. He gains a sense of security and reassurance from possessing it but also feels guilty about keeping it and worries that it will lead to his downfall.

Similarly, Theo invests Pippa with far more significance than any one person could live up to. She is the reason Theo lingers in the gallery before the explosion and therefore inadvertently saves his life. She is also the vessel Theo pours all of his love and yearning for his mother into.

Although the loss of his mother drives much of Theo's motivation and actions, there are clues to pre-existing flaws in his character. Before the story begins, Theo's early academic promise (prompting him to be placed in the same league as nerdy genius Andy Barbour) has already fizzled out. He has also taken up with Tom Cable, a friendship built solely on a shared love of risk-taking, leading to sprees of petty theft. Theo's appetite for self-destruction is already apparent and is only accentuated when his mother dies.

Although seemingly unable to conquer them, Theo is acutely conscious of his self-destructive tendencies. He declares himself "unfit" for any kind of hard work after his years of drinking and drug-taking in Vegas and admits his foray into antiques fraud was motivated more by his thrill-seeking nature than the need for money. This self-awareness leads to periods of deep self-loathing for Theo. In particular, he is haunted by Xandra's assertion that he and his father are very similar. Theo clearly recognises his father's conniving and deceitful character in himself when he tells a succession of lies to Hobie. He is also conscious of the parallels between the life choices his father makes and his own. His father's decision to leave his wife and son for a life gambling on the Strip is not so different to Theo risking the secure and happy life he has found with Hobie by committing fraud.

Theo's fear of turning into his father is aggravated by his increasing physical resemblance to him. He begins to see his father's face when he looks in the mirror and realises when he sees his father in an early film role that they could be twins. Despite loathing the characteristics they share, Theo is devastated when he learns from Mr Bracegirdle that the money in his savings account could have saved his father's life after all.

As the story progresses, Theo's inability to face up to the consequences of his actions lead to periods of feverish illness when events 'catch up' with him. His life slides into inevitable chaos as he loses control of almost every aspect of it. In a letter to Hobie, Theo compares himself to an abandoned dog that he and his mother once took in. Like the dog, which was too sick to save and destroyed much of the apartment before it died, Theo believes himself to be a hopeless cause and a destructive force in the lives of anyone who tries to help him.

During his visit to Amsterdam, Theo comes to a positive turning point in his life. Trapped in his hotel room after killing Martin, he believes he has finally reached rock bottom and attempts suicide. After seeing his mother in a dream, however, he experiences an epiphany, and realises the time has come to stop running and face the consequences of his actions. His decision to take responsibility for his life comes with the realisation that he does not have to turn into his father and that he may possess some of his mother's qualities.

Audrey Decker

Although Theo's mother, Audrey, dies at the beginning of the novel, her presence is felt throughout it. Half Irish and half Cherokee, she is warm, vivacious, intelligent and elegant.

When she was a girl, Audrey's parents died and she spent an unhappy childhood living with her fanatically religious Aunt Bess. It was during this time that she fell in love with a photograph of "The Goldfinch" in an art book. As a teenager, she moved to New York where she worked to put herself through an Art History degree at NYU. When she met Theo's father, she gave up her masters degree, along with her dreams of going on to do a PhD.

Larry Decker

Theo's father is, at first, notable in the novel for his absence, having abandoned Theo and his mother for a life in Las Vegas with his girlfriend Xandra. When Audrey is killed, the police are unable to trace him, making Theo, in effect, an orphan.

Ironically, when his father unexpectedly reappears to claim him, this is a disastrous moment for Theo. Although his father has admittedly changed, the transformation is from alcoholic, unpredictable, failed actor to a sluggish, self-medicating gambler.

After dragging Theo away from the Barbours to live in Las Vegas, Larry fails to look after his son, leaving him alone for days at a time. Finally, we learn that his true motivation for claiming Theo was to access the savings account that Audrey set up for her son. The debts that Larry has accrued are so large that only Theo's money can save him. His true nature emerges in the shocking scene where he punches Theo, forcing him to call his mother's solicitor to ask for money.

Larry dies as he lives: drunk and semi-conscious he veers onto the wrong side of the highway and collides with a tractor-trailer. Considering his irresponsible nature it is hard to say whether it is a deliberate case of suicide, or simply misadventure. Either way, he was clearly in the process of, once again, running away from his responsibilities.

Even after his death, his father's image is a warning to Theo of what he may become. He is uncomfortably aware that he shares some of his father's self-destructive and irresponsible impulses.

Grandpa Decker and Dorothy

Theo's paternal grandparents have never shown any interest in Theo and make it clear that they have no intention of taking him in after his mother dies. They remain similarly unmoved after the death of his father, failing to come to the funeral. Theo's father claims that Grandpa Decker was abusive towards him as a boy and that he and his stepmother, Dorothy, openly hated one another. When Larry was arrested as a youth they disowned him.

Pippa

Theo's glimpse of Pippa's bright red hair and golden eyes is the chance encounter that saves his life on the day of the explosion. He recognises that her thin, sharp features are not classically beautiful but sees something arresting in her, causing him to linger in the gallery.

Pippa is an orphan, cared for by her Uncle Welty after her mother dies. A brilliant musician, she is on her way to audition for the Juilliard when Welty takes her into the museum to see "The Goldfinch." Like Theo, Pippa suffers from post-traumatic stress disorder after surviving the explosion and even stops growing. She also suffers horrific physical injuries which leave her fine motor skills permanently impaired. Her Aunt Margaret sends her to a special needs boarding school in Switzerland and although she leads a normal life in every other way, Pippa has to face the fact that she will never be a professional musician. She also blames herself for Welty's death, as she asked him to accompany her to the audition that day.

Theo's fascination with Pippa is reminiscent of two other great literary obsessions: Jay Gatsby's love for Daisy in *The Great Gatsby* and Pip's hopeless adoration of Estella in *Great Expectations*. In both cases, love becomes obsessive when the loved one comes to represent much more than the sum of their parts. In the aftermath of the explosion, Theo's attraction to Pippa intensifies as his desire for her is intermixed with a range of more complex emotions.

For Theo, the fact that he and Pippa both survived the bombing links them inextricably. He also recognises his own psychological damage in Pippa's physical injuries. Significantly, Theo is more deeply attracted to Pippa when he sees her with her head shaved and metal staples over her ear shortly after her operation. He is also enthralled by the slight limp she is left with. Theo is also unable to separate his feelings for Pippa with the loss of his mother. As Pippa is present in the last moments Theo spends with his mother, she comes to represent the unspoilt life he believes he had before she died. Theo transfers much of his love and yearning for his mother onto Pippa.

While Pippa clearly has feelings for Theo, she gives him very little romantic encouragement. Theo is spurred on by the morphine-tinged kiss she gives him when they are teenagers, but in all probability, she does not remember it herself. She kindly but firmly brushes off Theo's further attempts to kiss her and returns the valuable topaz necklace he buys her, whilst keeping the first edition book. At the end of the novel, we learn that she does love Theo but believes that they are both too badly damaged to be good for one another.

Welty Blackwell

Welty was the business half of "Hobart and Blackwell." Charming and sociable, he loved networking and possessed an instinct for matching each antique with an owner who would appreciate it. After his death, the previously successful antiques emporium begins to suffer without his business acumen.

He is one of several characters in the novel who suffer under a tyrannical father. Tuberculosis of the spine leaves Welty a hunchback when he is a child and his bigoted father sends him out of his sight, to live with relatives in America.

Welty is the only one to show his half-sister, Juliet, any compassion. As she is illegitimate, Juliet is shunned by her father, her half-sister Margaret and even her own mother. As Welty is older than Juliet by 30 years, he brings her up like his daughter from the age of six. When Juliet dies, he does the same for her daughter, Pippa. His generous behaviour demonstrates that it is possible to break free of the cycle of parental abuse.

When Theo talks to Welty in the museum just before he dies, he feels a strong spiritual connection flowing between them. This feeling of affinity continues when Theo goes on to stay in Welty's old room. At the end of the novel, Hobie recognises that there is a further connection between them. He shows Theo an old photograph of Welty as a boy with a reproduction of "The Goldfinch" in the background. Like Theo, Welty became very attached to objects and their "souls" and spent his adult life travelling to see the original versions of the paintings he had loved as a child. On the day of the bombing, he had specifically visited the museum to share "The Goldfinch" with Pippa. Hobie suggests that, in his brief interchange with Theo, Welty felt those connections between them and gave him his ring to lead him to Hobie.

Cosmo

Welty's elderly terrier, Cosmo, is devoted to Pippa and sleeps in her sickroom when she is recovering from her injuries. When Theo returns after his period in Las Vegas, he discovers he has died.

Margaret Blackwell Pierce

Aunt Margaret is Pippa's closest remaining blood relative after Welty dies. She is the half-sister of both Welty and Juliet (Pippa's mother), as they all share the same womanising father but have different mothers.

The daughter of a Texan heiress, Margaret is a snob as well as a thoroughly unpleasant person. She refused to acknowledge Juliet as her half-sister, as she was sired by her father's affair with a hairdresser. Margaret insists on taking Pippa away from Hobie's where she is perfectly happy and sends her to a Swiss boarding school.

James Hobart (Hobie)

Like many of the characters in the novel, Hobie experienced a traumatic childhood. His mother died when he was a boy, leaving him in the hands of a sadistic, abusive father. Tricked into working for his father's trucking company without pay, he is saved by Welty, who offers him a job.

When Theo first meets Hobie, he reminds Theo of murals he has seen depicting Jesuit martyrs and there is certainly something saintly about him. He is an unworldly, gentle giant who forgets about the necessity of making money as he pours his love and attention into his beautiful restoration work.

Hobie's restoration skills are not only limited to his work with antiques. He is the saviour of the damaged and disowned, offering a refuge for both Pippa and Theo when their lives are cast adrift. Hobie is both a father and mother to Theo, providing the only sense of security and acceptance Theo experiences after the death of his mother. Theo feels that Hobie understands him far better than the professional psychiatrists, social workers or counsellors who are trying to help him. Theo's failure to confide truthfully in Hobie is his least forgivable mistake. Hobie nevertheless provides unconditional love and support even when Theo is at his duplicitous worst.

Andy Barbour

Andy is both a comic and a tragic figure. The misfortunes bestowed on him by nature are cruel and numerous: short-sightedness; multiple allergies; lack of physical co-ordination; monotone voice; nerdy manner and charisma bypass – to name but a few. Unsurprisingly, he is sadistically bullied, both at school and by his older brother Platt. He is even the least favourite child of his parents.

Theo forms an early alliance with Andy at school when they both become the targets of bullying for being academically gifted. Theo unceremoniously drops Andy, however, for the more dangerous and charismatic Tom Cable. Significantly, it is Andy that Theo first thinks of when social workers ask for a temporary address where he can stay. To Andy's credit, he shows no resentment at Theo's previous disloyalty and proves himself a loyal friend.

Life seems to look up for Andy when his genius earns him a fellowship in astrophysics. He also manages to acquire a Japanese girlfriend (a fact that particularly amuses Theo, as Andy was unhealthily obsessed with naked manga girls when they were teenagers.) Misfortune returns, however, when Andy dies in the way he most fears – whilst yachting with his father. Theo is horrified by the news of his death and feels guilty that, once again, he had let his friendship with Andy slip.

Samantha Barbour

A cool, elegant blonde, Mrs Barbour hails from a venerable Dutch family – the Van der Pleyns. When Theo goes to live with the Barbours, her cold, composed manner only serves to remind Theo of the warmth and vivacity he misses in his mother.

Mrs Barbour is full of contradictions. Whilst her kindness in taking Theo in cannot be denied, the lack of welcome in her manner makes Theo feel like a cuckoo in the nest. She spends much of her time fundraising for charity, but does not display that generosity of heart with her family. The luxurious Park Avenue apartment that the Barbours inhabit is an extension of Mrs Barbour's personality - beautifully staged but austere.

Mrs Barbour's transformation after the death of her husband and son is one of the most dramatic character developments in the novel. No longer interested in appearances, she spends her time propped up in bed in a room of ill-matching bric-a-brac. Her elegant couture has been replaced by pyjamas and dog-chewed slippers. Although grief has devastated her, it has also made her a nicer human being. Deeply regretting her failure to accept Andy for who he was when he was alive, she embraces Theo back into the family as a welcome connection to her dead son. Far warmer and more demonstrative with Theo than she ever was when he lived with her, she is thrilled when he becomes engaged to Kitsey.

Chance Barbour

When we first meet Andy's father, Chance Barbour, he appears to be a mild-mannered, reliable man whose life revolves around the Yacht Club and club sodas. So unassuming is his manner, that at times he seems almost "transparent."

Although Andy vaguely alludes to his father's mental health problems, Theo sees little sign of them when he lives with the Barbours. When Theo returns to New York and bumps into Mr Barbour in Central Park, his wild rantings and failure to recognise Theo are a complete shock. Only after the death of Andy and his father do we appreciate that Chance Barbour suffered from Bipolar disorder. During his youth, he was continually in trouble for unpredictable or dangerous behaviour, including arson, spending huge amounts of money, and incidents with underage girls. Medication and the stability of marriage had enabled him to be a good husband and father for a period, but a series of bad investments and an obsession with a young woman at work had brought on a relapse.

Chance Barbour loves to be near water, believing it is the source of all life. When he dies in a manic episode whilst he is sailing, it is both an ironic and fitting end to his life. Unfortunately, it also leads to the death of his son, Andy.

Kitsey Barbour

The Barbours' daughter, Katherine, is known as Kitsey to her family and close friends. When Theo is reintroduced to Kitsey as an adult, he is surprised to find that the annoying little girl he remembers has turned into an icy looking beauty and they quickly become engaged. Despite the fact that Kitsey is cheerful, beautiful and sociable, Theo sometimes has to remind himself of his good fortune. He is troubled at Kitsey's apparent lack of emotional depth and begins to suspect there is very little beneath her glittering surface.

When Theo discovers that Kitsey is in love with Tom Cable he is hurt and angry. On reflection, however, he is forced to admit that his own feelings do not run as deep as he would like them to. His relationship with Kitsey has been driven by a complicated mixture of motives: a desire to move on from his hopeless obsession with Pippa; a yearning to recapture the past and the wish to make Mrs Barbour happy again.

The revelation of Kitsey's true motives for becoming engaged to Theo shows the cool intelligence that lies beneath her disarming, fluttering manner. Over-involved in his own thoughts and feelings, Theo seriously underestimates her. When it comes to Tom Cable, she is capable of very deep emotions but is nevertheless determined to give him up for the sake of her family's happiness. While Theo believed she was disturbingly unmoved by the death of her father and Andy, she is, in reality, consumed by guilt. We learn that on the weekend they died, Kitsey sent Andy as her replacement, so that she could spend more time with Tom.

Kitsey is pragmatic in the way she regards her and Theo's impending marriage. Although they are not in love with one another she believes they will bring opposite and complementary qualities to the marriage. She is aware of Theo's drug habit and previously dissolute lifestyle, but believes they will keep each other on the straight and narrow. While Theo is shocked at her clear-eyed choice of head over heart, her argument makes a great deal of sense.

Platt Barbour

Platt is Andy's older and better looking brother. An unpleasant mix of sulkiness and aggression, "Platypus" is inexplicably Mrs Barbour's favourite child. While Theo is living with them, he is responsible for the hostility Andy's other siblings feel towards Theo, suggesting he may be a thief. Thankfully for Theo, Platt is away at school for the majority of the time that he lives with the Barbours. Towards the end of his stay, however, Platt is expelled from school for unknown reasons.

When Theo encounters Platt years later, he is unrecognisable. His handsome features have gone to seed and he wears a permanent air of down-at-heel anxiety. He has failed to live up to the expectation that he would be a successful businessman and works for an obscure academic publisher.

Although his life has been torn apart by the death of his father and brother, Platt clearly still harbours a great deal of bitterness and resentment. When he tells Theo about his father's illness, Platt cannot conceal flashes of his old aggression as he explains this is the reason he was unwillingly packed off to boarding school. He also claims to feel guilty for his sadistic bullying of Andy when they were children but still makes vicious comments about his dead brother at unguarded moments. He is clearly in financial trouble and attempts to sell Theo some of his mother's antiques without her knowledge.

Todd Barbour

Todd is the youngest of the Barbour boys. When Theo meets him again as an adult, he is bright, charming and successful - the antithesis of his brother, Platt. Todd tells Theo that his desire to work with disadvantaged young people was inspired by the time when Theo came to live with them.

Tom Cable

Theo views Tom as his best friend before his mother dies. There are echoes of Theo's later relationship with Boris in this early friendship. The boys recognise a wild and self-destructive streak in one another and while Tom is always the ringleader, Theo willingly accompanies him on sprees of petty thievery from empty holiday homes. Theo's appointment with the headmaster on the day of the bombing is the result of being seen with Tom while he was smoking.

Tom heartlessly avoids Theo after his mother dies, bringing their friendship to an abrupt end. He reappears in his life later on, when Theo discovers that Kitsey has been seeing him behind his back. The rest of the Barbour family strongly disapprove of Tom as he has been in trouble with the police, lives on credit and cannot hold a job down. There are also implications that he is unfaithful to Kitsey.

Enrique, Mrs Swanson and Dave

Well-meaning but ineffectual, this team of professionals all attempt, but fail, to help Theo come to terms with his mother's death. Enrique is Theo's social worker, Dave is his psychiatrist and Mrs Swanson, the school counsellor who advises him to throw ice cubes at a tree to express his grief.

Mr Beeman

Mr Beeman is Headmaster of the school Theo is attending when his mother dies. Audrey and Theo are on their way to discuss Theo's suspension with him on the day of the bombing.

Jose and Goldie

Good-hearted and exuberant, Jose and Goldie are the doormen who work at Sutton Place when Theo and his mother live there. Devoted to Theo's mother, who was kind to them, they look out for Theo after her death. They secretly store "The Goldfinch" for Theo when his father reappears and present him with some money that they claim Goldie owed his mother.

The two doormen become one of the very few certainties in Theo's life, as he has known them since he was very young and they are a connection with his mother. Theo is devastated when he goes back to Sutton Place and finds it has been demolished, as he realises he has no way of locating them.

Xandra

Theo cannot believe his eyes when he meets Xandra, the gum-chewing, chain-smoking replacement for his mother. Brash and cheap-looking, she is the complete antithesis of the beautiful, elegant Audrey. The contrast between the two women is highlighted through their choice of reading material: while Audrey reads high-brow tomes on the Arts, Xandra favours Jackie Collins and books about astrology. Despite claiming he is unable to understand what his father sees in Xandra, however, Theo is far from immune to the raw sexuality she oozes. Where Audrey and Pippa are compared to delicate birds, Xandra's inherent toughness reminds Theo of a big cat.

Unsurprisingly, Xandra makes a very poor substitute for a mother. Lacking any maternal qualities, (reflected in her neglect of Popper), she largely ignores Theo's existence and makes little attempt to conceal her drug habit. She is not, however, an entirely unsympathetic character. Like Theo's mother, Xandra is also at the mercy of Larry Decker's hopelessly unreliable nature. It is she who holds down the regular job, managing a bar in a casino, while Larry digs them further and further into debt with his gambling. There is also something poignant about her inability to distinguish quality from glitz – demonstrated by the cheap trinkets she selects from Audrey's jewellery box in favour of the expensive pieces. Xandra's inability to distinguish the real from the fake is one of the reasons she believes in Larry and his schemes to make them rich. When he dies, she is left with the financial mess he has created. Her decision to take Boris in, despite the fact that he has stolen from her, demonstrates her loneliness.

Boris Pavlikovsky

Like Theo, Boris is a boy with no true home. When the two boys meet, his father's house is also in the 'ghost town' of Canyon Shadows, but he has previously lived in dozens of different countries, travelling around with his father's job. As a result, his accent is an eccentric mix of Australian with a hint of Transylvanian. Even Boris's nationality is indefinable, as his Polish mother lived near the Ukrainian border and his father is Siberian. He claims his spiritual home is Indonesia and longs to return there.

Also like Theo, Boris is an only child left in the hands of his abusive, alcoholic father after the death of his mother. Boris is unsentimental about the loss of his mother, however, claiming that she was an alcoholic who died when she fell out of a window.

The friendship between these rootless, motherless boys is touching and powerful. Although Boris is undoubtedly a bad influence on Theo, leading him into drunkenness and drugs, he is also the only person who loves and sustains him during his time in Vegas. Boris is full of contradictions. He is alternately open-hearted and deceitful; fun-loving and morose; loyal and unreliable. He is, by his own admission, a thief and steals "The Goldfinch" from Theo but is unfailingly generous with his own possessions.

Boris's confused sense of morality is partly due to his harsh upbringing and partly based on his realisation that goodness is not always rewarded (reinforced by his continual re-reading of Dostoevsky's *The Idiot*). His assault on Kotku is a perfect example of this. Although he genuinely loves her, he believes that his passionate jealousy justifies hurting her. Similarly, Boris sentimentally recounts the purity of his spiritual connection with Amber, a 14 year-old girl whom he was dealing drugs to. Boris is unaware of the irony in his story, oblivious to the fact that dealing her drugs sullies both her innocence and their relationship.

Boris's tendency to embroider the truth always makes it hard for Theo to determine which of his unlikely tales are factual. He claims to have been an alcoholic from the age of ten; to have narrowly escaped being sold as a sex slave in Ukraine and to have swum in crocodile-infested waters. When they meet again as men, the lines between truth and fiction become even more blurred as Boris explains away what has happened to him in the intervening years. He claims that he moved in with Xandra, made money dealing drugs to the rich kids at school and worked for Bobo Silver. When Theo assumes Myriam is Boris's wife, he denies it and shows him a photograph of his "real" wife, Astrid, a former Olympic ski champion who spends most of her time in Stockholm. Theo notes with suspicion that the photograph looks like some kind of advert and the blond children bear absolutely no resemblance to Boris.

Despite Boris's very casual acquaintance with the truth, however, there is an honesty in the way he lives that we cannot help admiring. He lives fearlessly, following his often errant instincts, without ever agonising over his actions and the consequences. In this respect, he is very different to Theo who is often immobilised by his own doubts and fears.

Mr Pavlikovsky

Boris's father, Mr Pavlikovsky, works in the vague area of "mining and exploration." He takes Boris around the world with him, but fails to care for him and leaves him alone for long periods. When he is drunk, he subjects Boris to vicious beatings which he is then remorseful for. Boris's claim that his father once beat a man to death down a mine is one of his more believable stories. After a shocked Theo witnesses Mr Pavlikovsky beat his son, Boris poignantly defends him, insisting that his father must love him as he could have left him in Ukraine with a neighbour.

Popper

Affectionately renamed "Popchyk" by Boris, Popper is Xandra's neglected Maltese dog: a ridiculous looking fluffball, allegedly won by Xandra in a raffle. When Theo first arrives in Canyon Shadows, he discovers his father and Xandra have left Popper home alone while they were in New York. This is an omen of the kind of parenting Theo will receive while he is living in Las Vegas. Their shared neglect forms an immediate bond between Theo and Popper, despite the fact that Theo considers Popper to be a "girl's dog."

Theo dislikes the way Popper is tied up all the time and he starts to feel responsible for him. The dog becomes the constant companion of Theo and Boris, demonstrating particular devotion to Boris. Only when Theo leaves for New York does he realise how important Popper has become to him. Whilst living with his father and Xandra, Popper is the only living being who has shown him both affection and unfailing loyalty (although Boris is undoubtedly affectionate, his loyalty wavers according to his circumstances.) Rather than leave him in Vegas, Theo endures a tense and arduous journey to New York on the Greyhound with Popper concealed in a shopping bag. When Boris and Theo are reunited years later, Popper and Boris also enjoy a comically joyful reunion.

Kotku Hutchins

Kotku is the affectionate name Boris gives his first serious girlfriend. Theo is never entirely sure of her real name but believes it is something like Kylie or Kaylee. She is three years older than Boris and Theo finds her rather scary, with her Gothic make-up, air of worldliness and reputation for fighting other girls. Boris is besotted with her and his desire to spend every waking minute with her changes the dynamics of his friendship with Theo. Over-reliant on Boris's company, Theo once again finds himself unbearably lonely.

Although Kotku is not an immediately likeable character, we gain sympathy for her as we learn more details about her life. Her father is dead and she lives in a seedy motel on the highway with her mother. In the past, she has lived on the street and sold sexual favours to survive but has returned to school to finish her education.

Naaman Silver

Known to his associates as 'Bobo,' Mr Silver's exact occupation is never revealed. When Theo first meets him, he is struck by his extraordinary toupee and his eccentric dress sense (part-cowboy, part-lounge singer.) His breezy charm somehow accentuates the menace that lies beneath it. When Theo's father realises he cannot pay back his debt to Silver, he has a breakdown and dies driving up the wrong side of the highway.

After Theo leaves for New York, Boris works as Silver's assistant. Silver becomes a mentor and father figure to Boris, presumably teaching him a great deal about how to make money in the underworld.

Stewart and Lisa

The outwardly respectable "friends" of Xandra's who visit after Larry dies. Boris reveals to Theo that they were loaning Xandra money to deal drugs and turned on her when she couldn't pay them back.

Janet

Janet is Xandra's unreliable dogsitting friend who forgets to let Popper out while Xandra is in New York.

Mr Bracegirdle

George Bracegirdle is the solicitor hired by Theo's mother to take care of her will and financial affairs. He protects the savings account that Audrey sets up for Theo from Larry Decker's attempts to access it.

Elegant, cultured and intelligent, he had a great deal in common with Theo's mother and clearly adored her. Theo wonders whether there may have been more to their relationship than just friendship.

Everett

Pippa's English boyfriend, Everett, is a Music Librarian and shares a flat with her in London. Unfailingly cheerful, polite and inoffensive he is nevertheless loathed with a passion by Theo. The complete antithesis of Theo, he offers Pippa a sense of safety and stability.

Daisy Horsley

A casual girlfriend of Theo's who looks like Carole Lombard and already has a fiancé.

Mrs DeFrees

Moira DeFrees is an amiable, elderly lady who has an enigmatic relationship with Hobie, which may or may not be romantic. She and Hobie regularly go to dinner together and even spend weekends at her house in Connecticut. Theo later learns, however, that she is neither a widow nor a divorcee and is therefore presumably still married to her husband.

Grisha

A Russian Jew, Grisha works for Hobie, helping with removals and storage. It is also implied that he is involved in less salubrious business dealings completely unconnected to Hobie. Despite his considerable paunch, which occasionally forces his shirt buttons to pop open, he carries himself with the swagger of a movie star. It is on a visit to Hobie's storage unit with Grisha that Theo gets the idea to sell Hobie's pastiches off as valuable antiques and to transfer "The Goldfinch" to a storage unit.

Mr and Mrs Vogel

Hobie believes the Vogels to be his friends. Grisha, however, refers to them as "the Vultures" as they take advantage of Hobie's generosity, buying valuable antiques from him scandalously cheaply. The couple take an immediate dislike to Theo when he takes over the shop as he deliberately raises the price of everything he anticipates they may want to buy.

Anne de Larmessin

Kitsey's high society godmother hosts Theo and Kitsey's engagement party and takes charge of the organisation of their wedding. Her involvement is ironic as she clearly believes Kitsey is marrying beneath her.

Lucius Reeve

Reeve is the character who threatens to be Theo's undoing. Theo is blindsided when Reeve reveals he knows about his theft of "The Goldfinch." His perpetual presence in the background is a source of increasing anxiety for Theo.

Hobie knows Reeve as "Lucian Race" – a criminal who stole antiques from elderly people, but disappeared before he could be tried. He remains a mysterious, shadowy figure throughout the novel and it is perhaps no coincidence that his Christian names (Lucius/Lucian) bear a striking similarity to Lucifer.

Havistock Irving

Irving is present at the engagement party and is in conversation with Mrs Barbour when Theo first meets him. He introduces himself as an associate of Lucius Reeve and makes it clear he is aware of Theo's antiques forgeries and also his theft of "The Goldfinch". Mrs Barbour is acquainted with him as he volunteers at the New York Historical Society. Hobie, however, recognises him from 30 years previously when he went by the name of "Sloane Griscam." Hobie explains that he was a "knocker" (a term used in the antiques trade for fraudsters who steal from or cheat the elderly). Griscam was Lucian Race's partner in crime and Hobie and Welty testified against them. While Race disappeared, Griscam was sent to jail.

Myriam

When Boris appears in New York, the sinuous Myriam is his mysterious companion. Boris claims that she is his "right-hand man" and not his girlfriend. Whatever the truth, she is clearly an astute woman and Boris relies heavily on her judgement.

Horst

A German drug addict, Horst is an ambiguous and intriguing character. Boris perceives him as a tragic figure. He explains to Theo that Horst comes from a very wealthy family but lost everything when he became an addict. Boris's story is borne out when they visit his once grandiose townhouse which has fallen into decay and become a residence for junkies.

Like several of the characters, he deals in stolen art and forgeries but his discussions with Theo reveal intelligence and a shared passion for art. Horst greatly admires "The Goldfinch" for its artistic merit as well as its value and, like Theo, and Welty before him, first saw the painting when he was a boy. Although Boris trusts Horst implicitly, his true involvement in the disappearance of "The Goldfinch" is never clarified. He is certainly responsible for sending the assassins, Frits and Martin, to retrieve the painting but claims he would not have done so if he knew that it was Theo and Boris who had taken it.

Ulrika

Horst's on-and-off girlfriend, Ulrika is reportedly responsible for Horst's drug addiction and returns to him only when she needs money. Horst's masochistic devotion to her is all the more surprising when we learn from Theo that she looks like an eccentrically dressed "camel."

Sascha

Although we never meet Sascha in person, he is frequently referred to by the other characters. He is Ulrika's brother and Horst's "business" associate within the world of art theft. Boris believes that Sascha has been double-crossing Horst and using "The Goldfinch" as collateral for his own private deals. When the painting is finally retrieved after Boris's anonymous tip-off, Sascha is arrested.

Gyuri and Anatoly

Boris's Russian drivers.

Victor Cherry & Shirley T

Both work for Boris's shady underworld organisation. Although they are clearly no strangers to illegal transactions and even murder, there is an implicit sense of trust and loyalty between Boris and his "employees."

Martin and Frits

Theo is fooled by the harmless appearance of these two middle-aged American men until it becomes clear that they are assassins hired by Horst. We learn from Boris that Martin is certifiably insane and first met Horst in a psychiatric hospital.

Martin and Frits succeed in retrieving the painting from Theo and Boris, but Frits is shot by Boris and Martin is killed by Theo. Theo feels terrible remorse for shooting Martin, but Boris assures him that he has rid the world of an evil man.

The Asian Boy

Boris identifies the Asian boy who is present at both the Purple Cow Café and the shooting of Martin and Frits as Sascha's boyfriend. His real name remains uncertain but Boris thinks it may be "Woo" or "Goo." He takes the opportunity to steal "The Goldfinch" back after Theo shoots Martin.

8 - QUESTIONS FOR DISCUSSION

1/ Discuss how Tartt manages to create a timeless feel in the novel. Is the Dickensian tone at odds with its contemporary setting?

2/ Theo believes that it is purely his mother's death that catapults his life into disaster. There are signs, however, that he was going off the rails even before this point. Does Theo have a fatal character flaw? If so, what is it?

3/ When Theo walks out of the museum with "The Goldfinch," he has made a split second decision based on the instructions of a dying man. It is an impulsive action rather than a considered theft. Once Theo makes up his mind to keep the painting, however, he becomes culpable. How do we judge Theo over this? Does the recovery of the other artworks at the end of the novel justify his actions?

4/ Discuss the different things "The Goldfinch" represents to Theo and why he finds himself unable to give it up.

5/ Theo and Welty share a moment of spiritual connection in Welty's dying moments. What is it that they recognise in one another? Why do you think Welty gives Theo his ring and tells him to take "The Goldfinch"?

6/ Theo's sense of rootlessness is reflected in the different geographical locations he moves to. Discuss how Theo perceives each location (New York, Las Vegas and Amsterdam.) In what way does his perception of place mirror his own state of mind?

7/ Boris is wonderfully charismatic but he is also a bad influence on Theo. Their friendship leads Theo into drug addiction and even prompts him to kill a man. Does Boris enrich Theo's life or ruin it?

8/ Theo's love for Pippa is wrapped up with a yearning to return to life before his mother died. He is also attracted to her 'damage.' Discuss what Pippa signifies to Theo and whether he ever sees her for who she truly is.

9/ Of all the characters in the novel, Mr and Mrs Barbour undergo the most startling character developments. Discuss how they change and why.

10/ Theo's major motivation in becoming engaged to Kitsey is to please Mrs Barbour. Why do you think this is so important to Theo?

11/ Is Theo justified in feeling betrayed by Kitsey's affair with Tom Cable?

12/ An ongoing debate within the novel concerns whether it is better to follow your heart or your head. Discuss the different life choices the characters make in relation to this question. Does following your heart ensure happiness? Do you think Theo should marry Kitsey or continue to pursue Pippa?

13/ One of Theo's greatest fears is that he will turn into his father. Discuss the similarities between them and any differences.

14/ The "Amsterdam" section of the novel involving gangsters, double-dealing and shoot-outs, is very different in plot and pace from the previous parts. Did this shift in pace and mood work?

15/ Re-read the final few passages of the novel. How did they make you feel? Did you find the ending satisfying?

9 - QUICK QUIZ

Questions

How many of the following trivia questions can you answer correctly? Answers can be found on page 56:-

Q1/ Where are Theo and his mother going when they stop off at the museum?

Q2/ What is Pippa carrying when Theo first sees her?

Q3/ What did Theo's mother study at college?

Q4/ Where do Grandpa Decker and Dorothy suggest Theo could stay after his mother dies?

Q5/ What does Theo's first kiss from Pippa taste of?

Q6/ What is the name of Welty's elderly terrier?

Q7/ What is the housing development called where Theo's father and Xandra live?

Q8/ What nickname does Boris give Theo and why?

Q9/ Which film star does Theo's father blame for his failed acting career?

Q10/ How does Theo's father die?

Q11/ When Boris steals "The Goldfinch" from Theo's locker, what does he replace it with?

Q12/ What does Boris have tattooed on his arm in an attempt to convince Bobo Silver he is Jewish?

Q13/ What illness does Mr Barbour suffer from?

Q14/ What gifts does Theo leave in Pippa's boots when he leaves for Amsterdam?

Q15/ What prevents Theo from returning to New York after the shootout in Amsterdam?

Answers

A1/ To an appointment with Theo's headmaster

A2/ A battered flute case

A3/ Art history

A4/ A Holiday Inn

A5/ Morphine

A6/ Cosmo

A7/ Canyon Shadows

A8/ Potter because his glasses make him look like Harry Potter

A9/ Mickey Rourke

A10/ He collides with a tractor-trailer on the wrong side of the highway when drunk

A11/ His Civics textbook

A12/ A Star of David

A13/ Bipolar disorder

A14/ A first edition of *Ozma of Oz* and an antique topaz necklace

A15/ Boris has disappeared with his passport

10 - FURTHER READING

Donna Tartt and her Influences

Neither of Tartt's previous novels will disappoint. Also well worth reading are the classics that directly influenced *The Goldfinch*.

Great Expectations, Charles Dickens (1861)

The Great Gatsby, F. Scott Fitzgerald (1925)

The Catcher in the Rye, J.D. Salinger (1951)

The Secret History, Donna Tartt (1992)

The Little Friend, Donna Tartt (2002)

Other 'Dickensian' Writers

If you loved the epic sweep and timeless mood of *The Goldfinch*, the following contemporary novels are similarly 'Dickensian' in style. John Irving's novel, set in a Maine orphanage, has parallels to *Oliver Twist*, while *Jack Maggs* is Peter Carey's reworking of *Great Expectations*, written from the perspective of a convict returning from Australia to find his son.

The Cider House Rules, John Irving (1985)

The Quincunx, Charles Palliser (1989)

Jack Maggs, Peter Carey (1997)

The Crimson Petal and the White, Michael Faber (2002)

Fingersmith, Sarah Waters (2002)

Other Bildungsromans

There are a vast variety of "coming of age" novels to choose from, but these are some of the best.

Jane Eyre, Charlotte Brontë (1847)

Oranges are not the only Fruit, Jeanette Winterson (1985)

All the Pretty Horses, Cormac McCarthy (1992)

The Secret Life of Bees, Sue Monk Kidd (2002)

The Kite Runner, Khaled Hosseini (2003)

Black Swan Green, David Mitchell (2006)

The Interestings, Meg Wolitzer (2013)

New York

Classics that capture the essence of the Big Apple.

Bright Lights, Big City, Jay McInerney (1984)

Martin Dressler: The Tale of an American Dreamer, Steven Millhauser (1996)

BIBLIOGRAPHY

Tartt, Donna. *The Goldfinch*, Little Brown, 2013

Stephen King. "Flights of Fancy Donna Tartt's Goldfinch." *The New York Times*. 10 Oct 2013

Boyd Tonkin. "Book Review: The Goldfinch By Donna Tartt." *The Independent*. 18 Oct 2013

Julie Bosman. "Writer Brings in the World While She Keeps It At Bay Donna Tartt Talks, a Bit, About The Goldfinch." *The New York Times*. 20th Oct 2013

Kamila Shamshie. "The Goldfinch by Donna Tartt."*The Guardian*. 27 Oct 2013

Alexandria Symonds. "Still life with bombs, drugs and PTSD: Donna Tartt paints a masterpiece in The Goldfinch." *The Observer*. 29 Oct 2013

Gina Bellafonte. "Holden Caulfield Redux. A Look at the New York Novel "The Goldfinch" by Donna Tartt" *The New York Times*. 28 Nov 2013.

David Gilbert. "Donna Tartt." *Vanity Fair*. Nov 2013

www.mauritshuis.nl

ABOUT THE AUTHOR

Kathryn Cope is a reviewer and author of The Reading Room Book Group Guides. She lives in the English Peak District with her husband and son. The Reading Room series covers a wide range of titles for book group discussion from F. Scott Fitzgerald's classic *The Great Gatsby* to Gillian Flynn's contemporary bestseller, *Gone Girl*.

52363552R00037

Made in the USA
Lexington, KY
12 September 2019